Let's Celebrate Our Jewish Holidays!

Alfred J. Kolatch

ILLUSTRATED BY

Alex Bloch

Jonathan David Publishers, Inc.
Middle Village, New York 11379

Library of Congress Cataloging-in-Publication Data

Kolatch, Alfred J.
   Let's celebrate our jewish holidays! / Alfred J. Kolatch: illustrations by Alex Bloch
        p. cm.
   Summary: Introduces the history and symbols of various Jewish Holidays, including
   Rosh Hashana, Yom Kippur, and Shavuot.
   ISBN 0-8246-0394-X
   1. Fasts and feasts—Judaism—Juvenile literature. [1. Fasts and feasts—Judaism.]
   I. Bloch, Alex, ill. II Title
   BM690.K635   1997
   296.4'3—DC21   96–49289
                                                                        CIP
                                                                        AC

Designed and composed by John Reinhardt Book Design

Printed in China

To
Gabriella

Contents

1

The Sabbath

Our Day of Rest

The Sabbath, or Shabbat as we call it in Hebrew, is the holiest day in the Jewish calendar, even more holy than Rosh Hashana and Yom Kippur. It is the only holiday mentioned in the Ten Commandments.

The Bible tells us that God created the world in six days and rested on the seventh. For this reason, we set aside the seventh day of the week as our day of rest, a time when we refrain from ordinary, everyday activities.

Celebrating the Sabbath

   Shabbat begins on Friday evening, just before sunset, with the lighting of the Sabbath candles. After returning from evening synagogue services, the family gathers around the table to recite the *Kiddush* prayer over wine, enjoy a delicious dinner, and sing lively Sabbath melodies.

At synagogue services on Saturday morning, the Torah scroll is removed from the ark and members of the congregation are honored by being called up to the pulpit. A different portion of the Torah is chanted aloud each week, until, by the end of the year, the entire Five Books of Moses have been read.

When three stars appear in the sky on Saturday night, we bid goodbye to the Sabbath with the *Havdala* ceremony. A young person holds the flaming candle aloft, while the head of the household recites blessings over wine and spices.

Now, rested and refreshed, we are ready to begin the new week.

2

Rosh Hashana

Birthday of the World

Each year, in the Hebrew month Tishri, usually during the month of September, Jews all over the world celebrate the beginning of a new year. In Hebrew, the name of this holiday is Rosh Hashana, which means "Head of the Year" or "Beginning of the Year."

Birthday of the World

Some people say that it was on the first day of Tishri that the world was actually created, and that is why Rosh Hashana is called the birthday of the world. To help celebrate this holiday of new beginnings, we send greeting cards and flowers to those we love.

The Book of Life

Rosh Hashana is a joyous occasion, but it is a serious time as well. In the synagogue, we pray for a year of good health and love and peace. We hope that God will listen to our prayers and write good things about us in the Book of Life. And just as God is judging us, we must judge ourselves. Rosh Hashana is the Day of Judgment.

Sounds of the *Shofar*

The *shofar*—which is a ram's horn—is sounded during the Rosh Hashana synagogue service. The piercing blasts of this beautiful instrument remind us that the Jewish New Year is a time to think about our lives. The sounds of the *shofar* encourage us to decide which of our actions of the past year make us proud and which bring us shame.

Shana Tova!

Before returning home from the synagogue, we greet each other with the words "Happy New Year!" Those who know Hebrew say, *"Shana tova!"* We hope in our hearts that the year ahead will be a wonderful one for our families and for all people everywhere.

Rosh Hashana Treats

At home we enjoy a special holiday meal. A dish of honey and sliced apple are placed on the table. As we dip the apple into the honey, we wish for a year as sweet as the honey that we are about to taste. Some of us also enjoy dipping a piece of *challa* into the honey.

Honey cake, honeyed carrots, and other sweet treats are Rosh Hashana favorites. The carrots, usually sliced to resemble coins, are a symbol of good fortune.

14

Two round *challot* (plural of *challa*) are placed on the Rosh Hashana table. The round shape reminds us that one year is now complete and a new one is about to begin. Sometimes each *challa* is decorated with a bird or a ladder made out of dough. These decorations express the hope that our holiday prayers will reach heaven and be answered.

We Are Thankful

New fruits of the season—such as apple, grapes, and pomegranates (depending on where we live)—are served on the second night of Rosh Hashana. Before eating them, we recite a special prayer of thanksgiving. We are thankful for being able to enjoy these delicious foods and for being able to celebrate this beautiful holiday, the birthday of the world.

3
Yom Kippur
Day of Atonement

Ten days after Rosh Hashana we celebrate the sacred day of Yom Kippur. In English this holiday is called the Day of Atonement, a day on which we "atone" for our sins. This means that as we think about the past year, we regret the wrong things we have done and promise not to repeat them in the coming year.

A Time to Fast

Yom Kippur begins in the evening, before it gets dark, and doesn't end until three stars have appeared in the sky the following night. During this entire time—about twenty-five hours in all—adults do not eat or drink. They concentrate fully on their prayers and on the special meaning of the day. Children who have not yet become Bar or Bat Mitzva do not have to fast on Yom Kippur, although many try to fast for part of the day.

Praying for Forgiveness

The first prayer recited in the synagogue on Yom Kippur evening is the *Kol Nidre*, which means "All Promises." The cantor sings this meaningful prayer three times, and everyone in the congregation is moved by the beautiful melody. The words of the *Kol Nidre* express the hope that God will forgive us for promises we have not kept.

The Final *Shofar* Blast

During Yom Kippur, the Gates of Heaven are open all day long so that people might enter and reach God through their prayers. Then, as night falls at the end of the long Yom Kippur day, the gates are slowly closed.

After the last prayers of Yom Kippur have been recited, a long blast of the *shofar* is sounded. Everyone leaves for home, hopeful that the year will bring health, happiness, and peace to the world.

❦ 4 ❧

Sukkot, Shemini Atzeret & Simchat Torah

Joyous Days of Fall

Five days after Yom Kippur has ended—in September or October—the Sukkot holiday begins. This harvest festival can be traced to the time when Moses led the Israelites out of Egypt after more than two hundred years of slavery. As a free people, they wandered through the Sinai Desert for forty years until they finally reached the Promised Land, which we today call Israel.

During their years of travel in the desert, wherever the Israelites stopped to rest, they built *sukkot* (plural of *sukka*) to protect themselves from the fiery sun and hot sands.

What Is a *Sukka*?

A *sukka* is a small hut with walls usually made of wood or canvas. The roof is made of wooden slats. These are covered with corn stalks or tree branches that are spread out so that just enough sunlight can shine through during the day and so that the stars can peek through at night.

A Family Affair

The entire family participates in building the *sukka*—either in the backyard, on the house porch, or sometimes even on the roof of one's home. After the walls and ceiling have been put in place, everyone begins to decorate the *sukka*. Children draw pictures and then hang them on the walls, along with colorful banners and balloons. They string together apples, pears, grapes, and all kinds of vegetables and suspend them from the ceiling, reminding us that Sukkot is a harvest festival.

Symbols of Sukkot

Besides the *sukka* itself, the most important symbols of the holiday are the *lulav* bouquet and the *etrog*. The *lulav* is a palm branch. *Etrog* is Hebrew for citron, a fruit that resembles a large lemon.

To make a *lulav* bouquet, we slide the *lulav* into a holder made from palm leaves. In one pocket of the holder, we insert two willow branches; in the other pocket, we place three myrtle branches.

Each morning of the festival, we hold the *etrog* in the right hand and the *lulav* bouquet in the left hand. As we recite a blessing, we wave the *lulav* in six directions: north, east, west, south, up, and down. By doing this, we are demonstrating that God is everywhere.

Sukkot Meals

The Bible says, "You shall live in *sukkot* [huts] for seven days." Therefore, many Jews eat their meals in the *sukka* and even sleep there. Those who are not able to build a *sukka* of their own gather either in the synagogue's *sukka* or in that of a friend to recite the *Kiddush* over a cup of wine.

Invited Guests

On Sukkot, besides our real guests, it is customary to invite some imaginary ones to join us in the *sukka*. These visitors are called *ushpizin*. On each of the seven nights of Sukkot, we invite a different imaginary guest to celebrate with us.

The Seven Guests

The imaginary guests are selected from the heroes of Jewish history.

On the first night of Sukkot, we invite Abraham to join us in the *sukka*. Abraham is first because he welcomed strangers into his home, just as we do on Sukkot.

On the second night, our special guest is Isaac, the son of Abraham and Sarah.

On the third night of the holiday, the imaginary guest is Jacob. His descendants became the twelve tribes of Israel.

The fourth guest is Joseph, Jacob's favorite son, for whom he made a coat of many colors.

On the fifth night of Sukkot, we invite Moses into the *sukka*. This great Bible hero led the Children of Israel out of Egypt so that they could become a free people.

On the sixth night, Aaron, the brother of Moses, is welcomed as our special guest. Aaron always stood at Moses' side and helped him.

On the seventh and last night of Sukkot, David, the king of Israel, is invited to join us. We choose David as the last of our *ushpizin* because he built the city of Jerusalem, where the Temple later stood.

‿◠ Shemini Atzeret ◠‿

In ancient times, to celebrate the Sukkot holiday, Jews traveled by foot or by horsedrawn carriage to the Temple in Jerusalem. There, they offered thanks to God.

After Sukkot, before returning to their homes, the pilgrims remained in Jerusalem for one more day. On that day, which is called Shemini Atzeret, meaning "Eighth Day of Assembly," special prayers were recited and sacrifices were brought in the Temple.

Today, Shemini Atzeret is celebrated as a separate holiday, although many people think of it as the eighth day of Sukkot.

Simchat Torah

Every Sabbath of the year, we read a portion from the Torah as part of the synagogue service. The day on which we finish reading the entire Torah and start from the beginning once again is Simchat Torah, which means "Rejoicing with the Torah."

Simchat Torah, which immediately follows Sukkot and Shemini Atzeret, is the most joyous of all Jewish holidays. To celebrate the occasion, children as well as adults are called up to the Torah. The children are honored as a group. They stand under a large *talit* (prayershawl) and recite the Torah blessings in unison.

When the Simchat Torah service is over, all of the Torah scrolls are taken from the ark and paraded up and down the aisles. Children march behind, waving flags and singing. Everyone joins in celebrating the Torah.

5

Chanuka

Festival of Lights

The story of Chanuka begins about two thousand years ago when Alexander the Great, king of Greece, set out to expand his empire. After defeating the neighboring nations, he conquered Egypt, Syria, and then mighty Persia.

At that time, Persia ruled over Palestine, which was the land of the Jewish people. After Alexander the Great conquered the Persians, he expelled them from Palestine and replaced them with an army of loyal Syrian soldiers.

Alexander Visits Jerusalem

Alexander was kinder than the Persian rulers had been. He did not force the Jews to worship idols and allowed them to practice their own religion. This pleased the Jews very much. When Alexander came to visit Jerusalem in 333 B.C.E., he was cheered and showered with gifts.

To demonstrate their love for the Greek king, many Jewish parents named their babies Alexander. Some Jews even learned to speak the Greek language, and others wore Greek-style clothes and adopted Greek customs.

When Alexander the Great died, two of his generals quarreled over who should control the countries he had conquered. The generals compromised, and eventually Seleucus ruled over Syria and Palestine, and Ptolemy ruled over Egypt. About one hundred fifty years later, King Antiochus IV, a descendant of Seleucus, became the new ruler of Syria and Palestine.

Life Under a Tyrant

Antiochus IV was a vicious king. He did not allow the Jews to study the Torah and forced them to eat the flesh of swine. He erected idols all over Palestine and demanded that the Jews worship them. Antiochus even built a statue of Zeus, the chief god of all Greeks, in the Temple in Jerusalem.

Syrian-Greek soldiers were stationed throughout Palestine to ensure that the king's laws were obeyed. But the Jews were defiant. They refused to follow the orders of Antiochus.

Antiochus Goes Mad

When King Antiochus realized that the Jews were ignoring his commands, he stormed the Temple in Jerusalem and defiled all of its holy objects, including the *menora*, a beautiful seven-branched candelabrum. The Temple was left in shambles.

Mattathias and His Five Sons

One day, the Syrian-Greek troops advanced on the small village of Modi'in, not far from Jerusalem. Mattathias the High Priest, head of the Hasmonean family, summoned his five brave sons. "We must stop Antiochus!" he declared. "Let's take up arms against this madman!"

Judah was the oldest and bravest of the five brothers, and he became the leader. He quickly sent word to all able-bodied Jews to join him. "Whoever is for God, come to me!" was Judah's battle cry. And many Jews came, brandishing their swords. But they were only a small band compared to the large and powerful army of Antiochus.

Judah the Hammerman

Judah and his men hid in the mountains, and whenever Syrian-Greek troops could be seen approaching, the small band of Jews came down and attacked. Judah was so strong that he became known as the Maccabee, which comes from the Hebrew word for hammer.

Judah the Hammerman struck sharp blows against the enemy, and gradually the Syrian-Greek forces of Antiochus were chased out of the small villages and large cities of Palestine. The Maccabees, as Judah's small guerrilla army was now known, recaptured Jerusalem and the Temple.

The Search for Oil

When Judah the Maccabee and his brave soldiers entered the Temple, they were horrified at the destruction that surrounded them. The Maccabees removed the idols and searched for the holy *menora*. When they finally found it, they saw that the *menora's* seventh branch, the Eternal Light, had been extinguished. The Eternal Light was supposed to burn continuously.

The Maccabees looked everywhere for oil, but whatever they found had been contaminated by the Syrian-Greeks. By chance, they came upon one small vial of oil that still bore the seal of the High Priest, but that vial contained only enough pure oil to burn for one day.

. . . But, miracle of miracles, the oil lasted for eight days!

And since then, to remember the miracle of the Maccabees, we celebrate Chanuka for eight days each year, usually during the month of December.

The Chanuka *Menora*

Whereas the candelabrum used in the Temple was seven-branched, the *menora* designated to celebrate the Chanuka holiday has nine branches, each of which holds a cup into which oil or a candle is placed. Eight of the branches represent the eight days of the holiday. The ninth is for the *shamash*.

What Is the *Shamash?*

Just as the seventh light of the seven-branched *menora* in the Jerusalem Temple was used to kindle the other six, so the ninth light of the Chanuka *menora* is used to kindle the other eight. The ninth light is the *shamash*, the "server." Since its function is only to serve the others, it is not counted as one of the official *menora* lights.

Chanuka Treats

After the candles have been lit each evening, we sing happy songs celebrating the great victory of the Maccabees. And then, as a reminder of the miracle of the small vial of oil that burned for eight full days, we enjoy delicious *latkes*—crispy potato pancakes that have been fried in oil.

In Israel, it is customary to eat donuts that have been fried in oil.

Chanuka Fun

After enjoying our *latkes*, we are ready to play the *draydel* game.

A *draydel* is a four-sided top. On one side is the Hebrew letter *nun*, which stands for the Hebrew word *ness*, meaning "miracle." On the second side is the letter *gimmel*, which stands for the word *gadol*, meaning "great." On the third side is *hay*, which stands for *ha'ya*, meaning "happened." And on the fourth side is the letter *shin*, for *sham*, meaning "there." Taken all together, the words mean "a great miracle happened there [in ancient Palestine]." In Israel today, the letter *shin* has been changed to *pay*, the first letter of the word *po*, meaning "here."

When the *draydel* is twirled and falls with the letter *nun* facing up, each of the players puts a coin or a candy into the "pot." If the *shin* faces up, only the spinner puts a coin or candy into the pot. If the *draydel* falls so that the *hay* shows, the spinner removes half the pot as his or her winnings. If the *gimmel* faces up, the spinner takes all and the game begins all over again. Of course, the object of the game is to win as much money or candy as possible.

Chanuka Gifts

Giving gifts on Chanuka adds fun and surprise to the holiday. In some families gifts are given to children each night after the lighting of the *menora*. Giving Chanuka *gelt*, which is Chanuka money, is also a popular custom.

6

Tu Bi-Shevat

The Nature Holiday

Shevat is the name of a Hebrew month, and *tu* stands for the number fifteen. Tu Bi-Shevat, "the fifteenth day of Shevat," is the first Jewish holiday to follow Chanuka. In Israel, beginning in late January, the weather gets warmer and the tree buds begin to swell. This is the time when we celebrate nature. Tu Bi-Shevat is our New Year for Trees.

In Ancient Palestine

Two thousand years ago, when Jews lived in Palestine, the land was covered with cedar trees and cypress trees, fig trees and olive trees, and all kinds of nut trees. When the Romans conquered the land, most Jews left the country. The Romans who remained didn't care for the land. They chopped down the trees but never planted new ones. The land became barren.

In Modern Israel

In 1948, when the State of Israel was formed and the Jewish people returned to the land, they began the difficult task of restoring the earth to its former fertility. The Jewish National Fund started a tree-planting campaign. Gradually, millions upon millions of trees were planted, and soon the soil was enriched once again.

In Israel today, Tu Bi-Shevat is celebrated by children going out into the woods with their friends or parents or club leaders. They have picnics, play games, and—most important—they plant saplings and shrubs.

7
Purim
Story of a Heroic Queen

Purim is celebrated four weeks before Passover, in the Hebrew month of Adar—usually in March. This holiday is based on the story of a heroic queen and how she saved her people.

The Purim Story

The story of Purim is told in the Bible, in the Book of Esther.

Many years ago, in a country called Persia (now Iran), Ahasueros was king and Haman was his prime minister. To celebrate the third year of his reign, and to show his great wealth, Ahasueros held a lavish celebration that lasted for half a year. Following the festivities, there was a week-long banquet to which all the people of Shushan, the capital city of Persia, were invited.

On the seventh day of the feast, when he was a bit drunk, Ahasueros ordered his wife, Vashti, to dress in her royal robe and sparkling crown, and to appear before the crowd so that all the citizens of Shushan might admire her beauty. Queen Vashti refused, making the king very angry. Ahasueros quickly consulted with his advisers and decided to conduct a search for someone to replace the disobedient Vashti as queen.

The King's New Wife

A beauty contest was held, and the beautiful, young Esther was chosen to be the new queen of Persia. No one, not even King Ahasueros, knew that Esther was Jewish.

An orphan, Esther had been raised by her older cousin, Mordecai, who continued to watch over her. When Esther was crowned queen, Mordecai was worried about her well-being. And so, he spent much of his time sitting outside the gates of the royal palace, hoping to learn what was taking place inside.

One day, Mordecai heard a rumor that two officers were plotting to kill the king. He notified Queen Esther, who immediately sent word to Ahasueros, thus saving the king's life. Ahasueros was immensely grateful, and he quickly noted the incident in his diary.

Haman's Plan

King Ahasueros was very pleased with Prime Minister Haman, and he decided to grant him even more power. This gave Haman a feeling of great importance, and he soon demanded that all the king's subjects bow down whenever he walked by.

Mordecai, an extremely proud Jew, refused to follow Haman's order. "I will bow and kneel only before my God!" he announced.

When Haman was told what Mordecai had said, he decided to kill Mordecai and all the other Jews in the kingdom.

To select the exact day on which to carry out this evil plan, Haman decided to draw lots (Purim means "lots"). The thirteenth of the Hebrew month Adar was the day chosen for the massacre. Immediately, the wicked prime minister began constructing gallows upon which to hang Mordecai the Jew. And then Haman selected for himself the finest, most graceful horse, on which he would ride through the streets of Shushan to celebrate the event.

When he learned of Haman's plot, Mordecai tore his clothes, put on sackcloth and ashes, and cried bitterly. "You must not keep silent!" he pleaded with Esther. "You must visit the king and have him stop Haman from carrying out his plan."

Without first asking permission, as was customary in the palace, Esther entered the king's presence and informed him of Haman's plan to annihilate the Jews.

The Plan Backfires

One night, when King Ahasueros could not sleep, he asked one of his attendants to bring out the Book of Records and read from it aloud.

When the servant came to the part describing how Mordecai the Jew had saved the king's life, Ahasueros asked, "What honor has been given Mordecai for this wonderful deed?"

"Nothing at all has been done for him," replied the servant.

At that very moment, someone was heard entering the palace.

"Who is there?" asked the king.

"Your Majesty, it is Haman," a guard answered.

"Good," said the king. "Let the prime minister enter."

As Haman approached, Ahasueros asked him: "What shall be done for a man whom the king wishes to honor?"

Which person would the king want to honor more than me? thought Haman.

"Let the man whom the king wishes to honor be dressed in royal robes, the kind worn by the king," the prime minister said to King Ahasueros. "Let the man mount the king's royal horse," he continued, "and let him be led through the streets of the city. And whoever shall see him shall cry out, 'This is what is done for the man whom the king wishes to honor!'"

"You have spoken well," said Ahasueros to Haman. "Quick! Bring out royal clothes and a royal horse and honor Mordecai the Jew. Do everything that you have suggested!"

Wicked Haman's face turned white. He had no choice but to carry out the king's command. And so, he dressed Mordecai in royal robes and mounted him on a royal horse. Then, completely humiliated, Haman took the reigns of the horse and led Mordecai the Jew through the streets of Shushan, exclaiming, "Thus shall be done for the man whom the king wishes to honor!"

Haman's Downfall

Embarrassed and disgraced, Haman then went home and told his wife, Zeresh, what had happened. Zeresh said to him: "Be careful! If Mordecai, who has gotten the better of you, is a Jew, he will surely overcome you."

Just then, messengers came to Haman to invite him to a dinner that Queen Esther was planning. The king, too, would be present.

At the feast, King Ahasueros turned to Esther and said: "My dear Queen, what is your wish? Whatever it is, it shall be granted."

"There is a plot afoot to massacre and exterminate my people and me," Queen Esther replied.

The king was shocked to learn that Esther was a Jew. He became filled with fury. "Where is the man who dared to hatch such a plot?" he demanded.

"There is the evil man," said Esther, pointing to Haman.

The king then learned that Haman had erected a gallows upon which he had planned to hang Mordecai.

"Impale him upon it!" ordered the king angrily.

The order was carried out promptly, and all the Jews of Persia were finally saved from the plot of the vicious Haman.

Reading the Megilla

On the holiday of Purim, the story of the Jews of Persia and how they were saved from Haman's plot is read in the synagogue from the Book of Esther. The entire book is written by hand on a parchment scroll, or *megilla*. The Scroll of Esther is called *Megillat Esther* in Hebrew.

At the Purim service, children and adults come "armed" with *groggers* and other noisemakers. And whenever Haman's name is read from the *megilla*, everyone turns their *groggers* and stamps their feet in order to express their contempt for Haman, the enemy of the Jews.

36

Gifts and Merrymaking

The Scroll of Esther tells us that Mordecai sent a letter to all the Jews of the kingdom of Ahasueros asking them to celebrate the great victory over Haman by having a holiday feast and by sending gifts to each other and to the poor. The tradition of sending gifts on Purim is known in Hebrew as *mishlo'ach manot*.

As part of the joyous holiday celebration, it became customary for children and even adults to dress up in costume (sometimes as characters in the Purim story) and have a jolly time. In Israel, a great parade with floats and banners is held in many cities.

Purim Pastry

One of the favorite Purim foods is the *hamantasch*, a triangular-shaped pastry with a pocket filled with poppyseeds or prunes or some other fruit.

Hamantasch is a German word meaning "Haman's pocket," and some people say that the pastry got its name because Haman stole money and stuffed it in his pocket. Others explain that *hamantaschen* (plural of *hamantasch*) are shaped like a triangle because Haman always wore a three-cornered hat. Whichever is true, *hamantaschen* are a tasty Purim treat!

8

Passover

From Slavery to Freedom

In early spring, four weeks after Purim, we celebrate Passover, the festival of freedom. This important holiday, which we call Pesach in Hebrew, marks the exodus of the Israelites (or Hebrews) from Egypt, where they were enslaved for hundreds of years.

Escaping the Famine

About two thousand years ago, the Bible tells us, Joseph, one of the sons of Jacob, had become the chief advisor to the King of Egypt. Jacob and his family lived in the land of Canaan, where there was great famine.

Joseph asked Pharaoh, as the king of Egypt was known, if he would permit Jacob and his family to come and settle in Egypt, where food was plentiful. Pharaoh agreed and the entire family of Jacob packed up their belongings and moved to Egypt.

A New Pharaoh

Years later, when Joseph and the Pharaoh who trusted him had both died, the new ruler of Egypt grew suspicious of the Children of Israel, as the entire family of Jacob was then known. They had grown in numbers and wealth, and the new Pharaoh worried that if Egypt was ever attacked, the Israelites might decide to fight on the side of the enemy.

Pharaoh Enslaves the Israelites

In order to keep the Israelites under his control, Pharaoh made them work in the hot sun, building pyramids and other structures. When the Israelites didn't move fast enough or work hard enough, they were whipped by their taskmasters.

Still, Pharaoh wasn't satisfied. He wanted to reduce the numbers and strength of the Israelite slaves. He therefore ordered that every new-born Israelite male child be drowned in the Nile River.

A Baby in the Reeds

When a Hebrew woman named Yocheved gave birth to a baby boy, she feared for her son's life. And so, Yocheved made a little basket out of reeds, placed the baby in it, then hid the basket in the bulrushes at the edge of the Nile River. Miriam, the baby's sister, kept watch over the child from afar.

One morning, when Pharaoh's daughter, the Egyptian princess, walked down to the river to bathe, she heard the crying of a baby. Soon she discovered the basket hidden among the reeds.

The princess picked up the infant and immediately fell in love with it.

This must be a Hebrew child, she thought. *Why else would the child be hidden in the river?*

Pharaoh's daughter took the child into the palace and raised him as her very own son. She named him Moses, meaning "drawn out of the water."

Moses Grows Up

When Moses became an adult, he learned that he was not really an Egyptian, but a Hebrew, one of the Children of Israel. From that moment on, each time he saw his fellow Israelites being mistreated by the Egyptian taskmasters, he became filled with anger.

Finally, when Moses could stand it no longer, he and his brother, Aaron, went before the king. "Let my people go!" they demanded. "Let my people go so they can be free to worship our God."

Pharaoh ignored them.

Again and again, Moses and Aaron pleaded: "Let my people go! Let my people go!"

Still, Pharaoh would not listen.

Moses Turns to God

Feeling helpless, Moses turned to God for help.

God instructed: "Go once again to Pharaoh and say to him, 'If you continue to refuse to free the Children of Israel, you and all of the Egyptian people will be severely punished.'"

Moses did as God requested, but once again Pharaoh paid no attention to him.

God then said to Moses: "Tell your brother, Aaron, to take his staff and stretch it out over the waters of Egypt."

Aaron went to the Nile River and stretched out his staff over the waters. Pharaoh and the members of his court watched in disbelief as suddenly the waters of the Nile turned to blood.

The fish in the river died, and a terrible smell arose from the waters.

But Pharaoh was not frightened by this horrible plague. He still refused to set the Israelites free.

So God sent a second plague, the plague of frogs. The whole land was overrun by frogs. Frogs were everywhere in the king's palace.

And then came a third plague, the plague of lice.

And then the plague of wild beasts, and then the plague of locusts.

Even after nine plagues had been sent upon the Egyptian people, Pharaoh still refused to let the Children of Israel go.

The Tenth Plague

God instructed Moses to warn Pharaoh that if he does not free the Israelites at once, he will send a tenth plague. The firstborn male of every Egyptian family, including his own, will be stricken by the Angel of Death.

God then instructed Moses to tell the Israelites to prepare to leave Egypt that night. But first, each family was to slaughter a lamb as an offering to God and to smear some of the lamb's blood on the doorpost of its home. When the Angel of Death would see the blood, he would *pass over* (that's how the holiday got its name) the home, thus sparing the firstborn of the Israelites.

Pharaoh Finally Gives In

When Pharaoh learned that his own firstborn son had died, he said to Moses: "Go, take your people, the Children of Israel, take your sheep and oxen, and leave my country!" Quickly, the Israelites gathered all their possessions and fled the land of Egypt.

But, suddenly, Pharaoh changed his mind. *Why had he let the Israelites go?* he thought. And so, he called together his warriors, and chased after the fleeing slaves.

When the Israelites reached the Sea of Reeds, the Egyptians could be heard approaching right behind them.

At that moment, God ordered Moses to raise his rod and hold it out over the sea. Moses did as God instructed. Miraculously, the sea parted and the Israelites were able to march through on dry land.

The Egyptians continued to pursue the Israelites. And by the time the Israelites reached the other shore, the waters began to come together again and the Egyptian army was trapped. As all of Pharaoh's warriors were drowning, the Children of Israel were on their way to the Promised Land.

Why We Eat *Matza*

When the order came to leave Egypt, the Israelite slaves didn't have time to finish baking the dough they had been preparing. Instead, they put the dough on their shoulders and carried it with them. Later, when they finally had a chance to bake the dough, it did not rise (leaven). This flat, unleavened bread was called *matza*. To this day, throughout the Passover holiday, we eat *matza* instead of bread.

Preparing for the Holiday

During the entire eight days of Passover (except in Israel, where the festival is celebrated for seven days) we do not eat any leavened food, which is called *chametz* in Hebrew. Not only do we not eat *chametz*, but we do not allow any in our homes during the holiday.

And so, in preparation for Passover, every home gets a thorough house-cleaning. We bring out special Passover dishes and silverware. And, of course, we go shopping for special holiday foods.

Setting the Holiday Table

On the first two nights of Passover, Jewish families gather together for a special service and meal called a *Seder*. At the *Seder*, we read from a book called the *Haggada*, which describes the entire evening's ceremonies and retells (*Haggada* means "the telling") the story of how the Jews escaped from their enslavement in Egypt.

The centerpiece of the *Seder* table is a large tray with six compartments. In each compartment we place a symbolic food that helps tell the Passover story. One of these foods is horseradish (*maror* in Hebrew), which reminds us of the bitter lives suffered by our ancestors in Egypt. Another is a mixture called *charoset*, which usually consists of chopped apple, ground nuts, cinnamon, and a dash of wine. *Charoset* resembles the mortar that the Children of Israel were forced to make in order to build the pyramids. The other four symbolic foods are *karpas*, a green vegetable; *chazeret*, a vegetable with a bitter tang; *zero'a*, a roasted bone; and *baytza*, a roasted egg.

Seder Highlights

Among the important moments of the family *Seder* is the recitation of the "Four Questions"—the *"Ma Nishtana?"*—by the youngest child present. This special selection begins with the well-known words, "Why is this night different from all other nights?" When the child finishes reciting the "Four Questions," the leader and all *Seder* participants answer the child by retelling the story of Passover.

Another highlight of the *Seder* comes after the festive holiday meal has been served and the search for the *afikomon* begins. This piece of *matza*—which either the leader of the *Seder* hides and the children look for, or which a child steals and the leader looks for—must be found before the reading of the *Haggada* can continue. If a child finds the *afikomon*, he or she is usually promised a gift for returning it to the leader.

The *Seder* ends on a happy note with the singing of popular holiday songs, including the favorite *"Chad Gadya"*—"One Only Kid."

9

Yom Ha-Shoah

Remembering Six Million

The twenty-seventh day of the Hebrew month Nissan—six days after the conclusion of Passover—has been set aside as a time to remember the six million Jews who were murdered by the Nazis during World War II. The German army carried out Adolf Hitler's orders to round up Jews from all parts of Europe and ship them to concentration camps, mostly in Poland and Germany, where they were forced to perform slave labor. In the end, most were murdered in gas chambers and burned in ovens.

This day on which we remember the victims of the Nazi horror is called by the Hebrew name Yom Ha-Shoah, meaning "Day of Destruction." In English, we refer to it as Holocaust Day.

In Israel, all places of entertainment are closed on Yom Ha-Shoah. The day is commemorated by laying wreaths and reciting memorial prayers at Yad Va-shem, a museum in Jerusalem where much evidence of what happened during the Holocaust is on display.

More than anything, on this day we remember those who perished and promise each other that *never again* will we allow such a catastrophe to take place.

10
Lag B'Omer
A Day of Miracles

The period between the second day of Passover and the festival of Shavuot is called the *Omer*. In Hebrew, *lag* stands for the number thirty-three. The thirty-third day of that seven-week *Omer* period is a minor holiday called Lag B'Omer.

According to legend, the great Rabbi Akiba, who lived in Palestine about two thousand years ago, was the principal of a school with many students. Suddenly, a mysterious plague broke out, and one by one many of his students died. Then, quite miraculously, on the thirty-third day of the *Omer*, the plague ended. Since that time, students all over the world—especially in Israel—celebrate this joyous day by going on picnics, shooting bows and arrows, and playing all sorts of outdoor games.

11
Yom Ha-Atzma'ut
Rebirth of a Nation

For close to two thousand years, very few Jews lived in Palestine. In 1897, a journalist from Vienna named Theodor Herzl began to dream of reestablishing a Jewish homeland in Palestine. He realized that Jews who were being persecuted in many European countries needed a place that they could call home. To achieve this goal, he created a Zionist organization and worked tirelessly to establish a Jewish state.

On May 11, 1948, Theodor Herzl's dream came true. The British, who then controlled Palestine, agreed to follow the United Nations decision that the country be divided into two parts. One part was to be Jewish, the other part Arab.

The Jews accepted this idea of "partition," but the Arabs rejected it, wanting the entire land for themselves. This led to a bitter war. The Arab nations surrounding Palestine sent in armies to wipe out the Jewish settlements. The Jews, who had fewer soldiers and weapons, fought fiercely and bravely, and in the end they were victorious.

On the fifth day of Iyar 5708—which in 1948 was May the 14th—the Jewish people declared their independence and established the modern State of Israel. At last, the Jewish people once again had a homeland.

Each year, on the fifth of Iyar, we celebrate the rebirth of the Jewish nation. This momentous day is called Yom Ha-Atzma'ut, Israel Independence Day.

❦ 12 ❧
Shavuot
Moses on Mount Sinai

Seven weeks after the first day of Passover, in late May or early June, we celebrate the Shavuot holiday. The festival of Shavuot ("Weeks" in English), which arrives when the wheat crop is ripe and ready for cutting in Israel, is one of our three harvest festivals.

Shavuot and Mount Sinai

Many years ago, Jews who lived in all parts of Palestine would bake bread from the freshly harvested wheat crop and bring the loaves to the Temple in Jerusalem as an offering to God. Later, when many Jews left their farms and moved to the cities, they no longer were able to celebrate the harvest festival in this manner. But the Shavuot festival was such a joyous one that Jews wanted to continue celebrating it.

The Rabbis studied the calendar, and they discovered that the sixth day of Sivan—the Hebrew date on which the Shavuot harvest holiday was celebrated—is also the date on which Moses received the Ten Commandments and the Torah from God on Mount Sinai.

From that time on, the Shavuot harvest festival became linked to the great Mount Sinai event, and the Shavuot holiday also became known as *Zeman Matan Toratenu*, "Time of the Giving of Our Torah."

Holiday Decorations

When Moses climbed to the top of Mount Sinai, he saw a blanket of lovely green trees and shrubs, as well as colorful wildflowers. To remind us of this exquisite scene, on Shavuot today we decorate our synagogues and sometimes our homes with all kinds of greenery.

Torah Study on Shavuot

In Israel, Shavuot is celebrated for one day, but in other countries it is traditionally celebrated for two days. After the first evening service of the holiday, many Jews gather to study the Torah and other holy books. Some study all through the night.

The Book of Ruth

In addition to the holiday Torah portion that is read aloud in the synagogue on Shavuot morning, we also read the Book of Ruth. Like the Book of Esther, which is read on Purim, the Book of Ruth is called a *megilla* because it was originally written on a scroll. The Scroll of Ruth tells the story of how the loyal, courageous Ruth met her husband, Boaz, at harvest time in the month of Sivan.

Shavuot Delicacies

According to an old legend, when Moses came down from Mount Sinai and gave the Torah to the Children of Israel, they wanted to hold a big celebration. Having little time to prepare an elaborate meat meal, which would require slaughtering an animal and making it ready for cooking, they prepared a dairy meal instead. And so, it has become customary on Shavuot to serve dishes made with milk, cheese, and other dairy products. It is popular to serve two cheese blintzes at mealtime as a reminder of the two tablets on which the Ten Commandments were written.

Another Shavuot holiday treat is *kreplach*, three-sided dumplings filled with cheese. The triangle shape of the *kreplach* reminds us of Abraham, Isaac, and Jacob—the Patriarchs of the Jewish people.

⟪ 13 ⟫

Tisha B'Av

A Day to Mourn

Solomon, the son of David, was king of the Jewish people about three thousand years ago. To honor God, he decided to build a magnificent Temple in the city of Jerusalem. King Solomon purchased strong cedar and cypress trees from the mountains of Lebanon and had them floated down the Mediterranean Sea. He hired thousands of masons to cut huge blocks of stone from the rocky mountains of Palestine. After seven long years of backbreaking work, the Temple was finally completed. King Solomon raised his hands to heaven and exclaimed:

Oh Lord, God of Israel,
There is no God like You.
We dedicate this beautiful house to Your Name.

About four hundred years later, in 586 B.C.E., the Babylonians invaded Palestine. On Tisha B'Av, the ninth day of Av, they burned the Temple to the ground.

About seventy years after that, the Jews of Palestine built a new Temple on the very spot where the First Temple had once stood. Then, in the year 70 C.E., again on the ninth day of Av, the Romans, who had conquered Palestine, destroyed the Second Temple. All that remained of the structure was the Western Wall, which sometimes is called the Wailing Wall because Jews go there to pray and pour out their hearts.

To remember these sad days in our history, the ninth day of Av has become a fast day for Jews the world over. In the synagogue, special prayers are recited and the biblical Book of Lamentations (Aycha) is read aloud.

About the Author

ALFRED J. KOLATCH, a graduate of the Teacher's Institute of Yeshiva University and its College of Liberal Arts, was ordained by the Jewish Theological Seminary of America, which subsequently awarded him the Doctor of Divinity Degree, *honoris causa*. From 1941 to 1948 he served as rabbi of congregations in Columbia, South Carolina, and Kew Gardens, New York, and as a chaplain in the United States Army. In 1948 he founded Jonathan David Publishers, of which he has since been president and editor-in-chief.

Rabbi Kolatch has authored numerous books, including several geared for young people: *The Jewish Child's First Book of Why*, *Classic Bible Stories for Jewish Children*, and *A Child's First Book of Jewish Holidays*. He is perhaps best known for his *Jewish Book of Why* and its sequel, *The Second Jewish Book of Why*. Other popular works include *This Is the Torah*, *The Jewish Home Advisor*, and *The New Name Dictionary*.

About the Artist

ALEX BLOCH is a graduate of the College of Scenic Art of Moscow and of the Institute of Printing Art of Moscow. Since immigrating to the United States in 1980, he has worked as a scenic artist on such films as *Beat Street*, *Moscow on the Hudson*, and *The Cotton Club*. Mr. Bloch has illustrated numerous children's book, including *Baby Brontosaurus*, *Baby Stegosaurus*, *Salmon County*, *Meet the Moon*, and *Abuelito's Going Home*. Mr. Bloch lives in New York City.